Looking for Boo

by Susan Blackaby

illustrated by Andy Levine

MODERN CURRICULUM PRESS
Pearson Learning Group

Bink had a gerbil named Boo. She was brown. She was fuzzy. And she was lost.

Where was Boo? Bink tried to guess. He looked all over the house.

"Boo is lost!" he said. "I have looked everywhere. I will never find her."

"Never say never," said Mom. "Look under your nose."

Bink looked under a bush. He surprised his dog. The dog was not pleased.

Bink looked under the house.
He surprised a fuzzy rabbit.
The rabbit was not pleased.

Then Bink looked under his nose.
Can you guess what Bink saw?
Bink was pleased. So was Boo!